aufactured in the United States

resemblance to actual events or persons, living or dead, is entirely coincidental. This is in orm meant for harm nor do we promote harm. Personal perspective use only. Please do not y/mimic any words or illustration from this book.

strations by Cameron Wilson for Soulsimplicity Design and Publishing.

To everyone who has been a part of my journey,

I want to express my heartfelt gratitude. The unique traits of my characters were inspired by the diverse personalities I've encountered throughout my life, each leaving a lasting impression on me. From moments of wisdom to displays of pride and everything in between, your influence has added depth and richness to my storytelling. They say it takes a village to raise a child, and I'm fortunate to have a wide network of people who have helped shape my path. Thank you for being a part of my village.

Dedicated to all those who dare to dream, may *'Sense Makes Change'* ignite within you the courage to embrace the transformative power of change. Remember, we can always better our best. Let this book serve as a beacon, urging you to approach life with intentionality and foresight, guiding every action with a clear vision of the end goal.

To Boobis, your unwavering support and invaluable contributions breathed life into my words when my creativity slowed down. Thank you for helping when I got writers block to lock in and give me fresh realistic ideas to help make my script come to life. Amidst the challenges, your insights and encouragement were the cornerstone of this journey. With deepest gratitude, I thank you for standing by me, amplifying the essence of *'Sense Makes Change'* to its fullest potential.

And to my great-grandchildren yet to come, may this be the genesis of a legacy woven with wisdom and insight. As you navigate life's test and experiences, may you learn lessons from every triumph and tribulation. Let each experience shape your narrative, and may you, too, immortalize your journey in the pages of time. Let 'Sense Makes Change' be the first of many echoes of our collective wisdom, resonating through generations to come.

-P. Hill

SENSE MAKES
CHANGE

PATRICK SHALON AMIN HILL

SENSE MAKES CHANGE

ACT I

Just about everything in life comes and goes. People are the same. There are many important people in our lives: our mothers and fathers, sons and daughters, brothers and sisters, aunts and uncles, grandmas and grandpas, and even our friends. One thing that we are all promised—those people included—is death. How or when death will come, we never know. We don't know until it happens.

But we do know that pain comes alongside death, always. That is what we call effect by cause. Every cause has an effect, and every effect has a purpose. That purpose is either a positive or a negative one. You choose which way you take such things.

You see, the God I serve makes no mistakes and doesn't give me more pain than I can handle. I didn't understand that until I was an adult. Now I realize that just about everything we do in life is a choice we've made, whether we believe that's the case or not. If you learn to conquer emotion, you learn to conquer action. Our actions are often based on emotions, and these emotions control our relationships. When our emotions are negative, negative things happen.

Which is why we're here today.

On this particular day, Chris and his friend Poppa decide to spend some time playing a video game together. It is the weekend after all, and there really isn't any better activity for some good friend bonding than NBA 2K.

"Uh…what up K.D. WET!" Chris hollers."Sike!" Poppa calls back. "He ain't Bron. Let's go!"

"Who winning though he got 25 on 'em…" Chris says with a sigh. "Man, I aint tryna hear that! You know they be cheating for him on here."

"Come on, Pop," Chris says, setting his controller down. "How long you gone use that excuse?"

"That's what's real, bruh!" Poppa shakes his head and begins on another tirade, but his phone rings. He glances over at his buddy. "Hold up."

Chris nods and returns to his controller. He pauses the game.

Poppa brings the phone to his ear. "Hello…Whats good, bruh? Yeah, I got you. How much change you need now lil man? Ight, fasho, I got you. I'm over here at the YDC GETTING BUCKETS!...Haha, but yeah, bruh, come by the center. I got

you on that…Bet."

He hangs up his phone and looks

back over at Chris. "Man, what was that?"

Chris says, eyebrow raised.

"That was me showing you how a

King dominates the court, baby!" Poppa

grins and goes for his controller once more.

Chris stops him. "Man, I'm talking

bout on the phone. Why you trying to bring

that stuff to the center? You know my pops

would kill us if he found out."

Poppa shakes his head, as though this

very thought is a joke. "Naw, Chris, Peezy

stay strapped."

He pulls a gun out of the bag to his left and cocks it, just for show. Chris can only see the handle, but he still holds up his hand in frustration.

"I'm being fareal, bro," Chris says, swatting Poppa's arm. "It's called the 'Youth Development Center' for a reason. The whole purpose of the center is to empower the youth and make a positive impact on our lives. You tryna bring negativity here?"

Poppa laughs, short and loud. "You sound like a mark. Negativity? Naw, lil man, this all positive."

This time, Poppa reaches into his pocket. He pulls out a stack of bills, only slightly, and Chris' eyes widen. They're all hundreds.

"Everybody can't live that suit-and-tie life," Poppa says by way of explanation.

"You going to sell yourself on that excuse?" Chris says.

"That ain't no excuse!" Poppa says, shoving the money back into his pocket. He stares down his friend. "My chance of that life was taken from me when I was 16 and decided to catch a lick on the pizza man. I was young and dumb. That decision got me three and a half years of strict confinement.

Now, here I am, 22 years old with a felony on my belt for something I did when I was a kid. You know how hard it is for a felon to get a job out here? The fast food joints don't even want you. The government put a sign on me that says I ain't worth shit. I have to eat. I have a family. I have a daughter to look after. I'm a man, and I'm gonna get it by any means."

Chris stares back, his expression completely calm. "I hear you, bro. All I'm saying is don't bring around my dad's business. He worked hard to get this. Have some respect."

Poppa nods, slow and solemn. It does make sense. "You right, and I feel that. My bad, G. Yo pops a coo dude."

As if on cue, the door behind them opens. Chris reaches over and elbows Poppa. "Put that gun away," he whispers urgently.

Poppa quickly shoves the end of the gun back into his backpack and reaches for his controller again instead. Just as he is able to unpause the game, Chris' dad approaches from behind the couch.

"What's up boys?" Mr. T says. He then notices his son's friend and smiles. "Poppa, is that you?"

"Yeah, what's good, Mr. T!" Poppa says, turning around to look at the man. "You know it's me!"

"What's up, pops?" Chris says. He reaches out to fist bump his old man. "Y'all staying out of trouble?" Mr. T asks with a small smile.

"All the time," Chris says quickly. Perhaps too quickly.

Poppa grins and shakes his head. "Boy, stop lying. Chris in trouble as we speak. I know you taught him better than this. He went looking for trouble when he picked up the sticks against me. Can't nobody see me in this 2K…"

Chris smacks his teeth in response, eliciting a chuckle from Mr. T.

"Good one," the man says. "Hey, how your mother and brother doing, Pop?"

Poppa turns around on the couch, so he can see the man. "They good. Mom's just made 42, and you know Mike living that superstar college life. He made All-American this past season. They have him picked to go first-round from his graduating class if he keeps making them plays." Mr. T grins. "That's good news."

"That's great news, Pop," Chris says, turning towards the pair also. "It hasn't been anybody from our area that went pro. He giving a lot of people reason to dream big."

Mr. T ruffles his son's hair with a laugh. "Yeah, you're right. I miss them days."

Before he can muse anymore, a scrawny boy of about sixteen walks in with a paper in hand. Poppa and Chris turn back around and continue their 2K in order to give Mr. T some privacy.

"Hey, Mr. T," the kid says, his voice shaky. "I was wondering if I could pick up some part-time hours with you this summer? I could really use some extra cash."

Mr. T takes a look at the paper and then back up at the kid before him. "Yeah, I'm sure we can find something for you. We could use some extra team leaders this summer."

The kid seems to let out an actual sigh of relief at this. "Awesome. Thanks.

When they hear the door close after the kid walks out of the room, Poppa speaks up again.

"Mr. T, how much you paying these folks to work here?"

Mr. T approaches and sits in a nearby chair, eyes also trained on the TV. "Minimum wage. Why? You need a job, Pop?"

Poppa scoffs, as though he can't even believe Mr. T would ask such a thing. "Minimum wage? You gotta be kidding me. What's that, like $7.25 an hour? Full-time, 40 hours a week, gone make me about $290.

So really like $210 after government taxes.

Nah, thanks but no thank you.

Ima stick to what I know."

Mr. T leans in, his arms crossed atop

his knees. "Where do you see yourself in

five years, Pop?"

Poppa shrugs. "I don't know. I

haven't really thought that far ahead. I live

for the day." Just then, Chris lets out a moan

of disappointment as Poppa dunks on him

onscreen.

Poppa stands in victory.

"Let's goooooo!"

Mr. T stands with Poppa and gets his attention once more. "Pull ya britches up, Poppa!

What do you wanna be in life?"

Poppa looks over at him, recognizing the mistake he's made in not providing an answer right away. He looks down at Chris and then back to his friend's dad. "My bad, Mr. T. I mean, if I'm not dead or in jail, I want to run my own barbershop one day."

Mr. T nods and shifts his weight back onto one leg. "If you surround yourself with positive people, death or jail won't be the first thing to come out your mouth. You are the company you keep. I suggest you find somebody who has what you want and let them teach you how to get what they got."

Poppa nods solemnly. "True, I feel that."

Mr. T watches Poppa's expression, trying to ensure his words are truly getting through to the kid. "Now, the barbershop idea sounds good. How do you plan on making that happen?"

Poppa shrugs, not meeting the man's eyes. "Keep getting heads cut, and go get my barber license."

"Now, that's a start. But it's gone take a lot more than that. You definitely have the potential, but you have to really want it. A lot of people have things they really want to do, but they never take the necessary action to make it happen. The only place where success comes before work is in the dictionary. You have to put in work. Do some research!"

"True," Poppa says. "I mean, I already know all that."

Mr. T lets out a quick laugh. "So what are you waiting on then?"

Poppa shakes his head and sits back down, pressing his back against the couch.

"Man, really I just need to hire somebody to put me up on game with the business side of it all."

Mr. T nods at this. "You can either have excuses or results. But you can't have both! I can help you if you do your part as well."

"I feel where you coming from, and I appreciate the talk." Poppa looks like he's about to say more, but he stops himself. "I'm fina get up out of here though. I'll catch up with y'all later."

Mr. T shakes his head with a gentle smile. "Alright, Pop, just remember what I said." "No doubt," he saus with a nod. He turns to his friend, who still sits with

controller in hand. "Ima get up with you,

Chris. Lucky ya pops came in and saved

you from that uh-"
"Boy, shut yo mouth,"
Chris retorts. Poppa does no more than

smile on his way out.

ACT II

Nikki gets dressed more quickly

than most, but it still takes time to look as

good as she does. On this particular night,

she makes it as far as putting her makeup

on before her phone rings.

It's her boyfriend. She answers

quickly and talks low, though she knows her

mom can usually hear every other word she

says from down the hall.

"Hey, babe…I'm almost done

getting dressed…Yeah, just pull up in front.

I'll be out in a sec…They downstairs, so

they probably gonna want to talk to me.

You know they leave tonight, and I'm sure

Daddy gonna want to give me one of his

speeches…Oh, no, no, I'm still having the party…What? No, don't even worry about it. I'll talk to you when I get in the car. Okay?...Bye."

The moment she sets her phone back on the table next to her, both of her parents are at her door. Of course they are.

"Nikki," her mom says, leaning against the door frame. "Are you sure you don't want to come with us?"

"I'm sure, Ma," she says as she finishes the wing of her eyeliner. "I don't even like going out there. Its too hot, and there ain't nothing to do."

Her mom sighs as she stands and moves towards the bed. She grabs her coat, her wallet, and her phone. The sooner she can get out of this, the better.

"Mom, I was in middle school," she says. "I'm a senior now. That doesn't excite me anymore."

Her dad laughs lightly at this, finally making himself known in the discussion. "The only thing that seems to excite you is this boy we've never met pulling up to pick you up every other night."

Nikki moves towards the door as quickly as she can, but her parents are both standing in the entrance to her room. She can't escape.

"Dad, stop. He's a good guy. You will meet him when y'all get back. Promise." She doesn't know why she promises, but she does. This gives both her parents pause.

"What kind of guy picks up a 17-year-old girl and doesn't meet her parents?" her dad asks, shaking himself out of his reverie.

"Yeah, Nik, and you don't even talk about college anymore," her mom says in kind.

Nikki glances at herself in the mirror again. The sooner she can get out of this the better. "Me not wanting to go to college anymore has nothing to do with him. You guys always think you know what is best for me. I'm not a little girl anymore."

This does absolutely nothing to diffuse the situation. Her dad shakes his head and squares up to his full height.

"Who knows what is best for you if we don't? Last time I checked, we were living good, eating good, keeping nice clothes on you, and giving you a nice area to grow up in. We done brought you 17 years of life with no worries, and you still ungrateful. There is a bunch of folks out there who would die to live your lifestyle, and you don't even realize it. My, my, my, kids these days." He turns towards her mom, who nods in approval.

Nikki can feel frustration bubbling up within her. "Daddy, stop it. I do appreciate everything you and Mom do. Its just…some things I want to figure out myself. I know college used to be one of our most-talked-about topics in this house. But now that I'm older, I don't feel like I need it to get where I want to be in life. I go there for four years, y'all spend about 40 thousand, and I still don't even have a for-

sure job when its all said and done."

Her dad sighs, his fight not

disappeared at all. "Nik, you are absolutely

correct. Nothing in life is guaranteed. But

we have to make the best of what we have.

Along the way, you meet other likeminded

people in the same field as you. If you have

great work ethic and personality, that will

take you where you want to be. It's not

always necessarily what you know. It's *who*

you know that will open them big doors for

you in life. Your mother and I just want

what is best for you. I was there at one

point, and I don't want to see my little girl there."

Nikki's heart softens at this, and her father's seems to as well. They gaze at each other for a long moment. "Aww, DDaddy..." she sighs. "I promise I won't let y'all down, alright?" Her mom smiles a tight smile.

"It's easier said than done, sweetie." "I know, Mom. Just watch."

And with that, they unobstruct her doorway. The family moves towards the front door, into the living room.

"So, what are your plans for the weekend while we are gone?" her mom asks as they walk.

"Not too much," she says nonchalantly. She really has no idea how much her mom heard of the phone call. The walls in this house are so damn thin. "I told Steph I would do her hair tomorrow. Other than that, I'll probably just go to the YC."

Her mom nods with approval. "Alright, well, stay out of trouble. And if you need anything, just give us a call."

"Will do," Nikki says as her hand goes towards the doorknob of the front door. "I hope y'all have a fun trip. Tell Auntie I love her and will see her soon. My ride is here."

The family exchanges "I love you"s all around, and Nikki finally closes the door behind her. In her wake, her parents look at one another.

"Our baby is all grown up," her mom says with a small smile.

Her dad though is quick to shut down this adoration. "No, that's the problem now. She thinks she's grown. Running around here acting like she know it all."

Her mom shakes her head. "Hmm…

well, I wonder where she gets that from,

honey."

Her dad lets out a slight laugh.

"Don't you start, sweetheart. You know I

have logical reasoning behind any and

everything I do or say. Nikki is just at that

stage in her life when she feels like she

knows it all. She doesn't realize how

beneficial we are to her."

Before her mom can come up with a

response of some kind, Nikki races back

inside, her phone in her hand.

"Did you forget something,

sweetie?" her mom says quickly, surprised

by the sudden appearance.

"No," she says quickly. She looks

down at her phone and then back up again.

"Well, yes. I was wondering if y'all could

leave me with some money for the

weekend? I wanted to grab a few things

while I was out at the mall. Please,

DDaddy?"

Her dad shakes his head

immediately. "Nope, talk to your mother. I

just gave you some money."

Nikki turns her gaze to her mom.

"Mom? Please?"

Her mom looks for her purse and finds it on the entry table nearby. "How much you need, Nikki?"

She hesitates for a moment, a clearly fake hesitation, and then says, "would be fine."

"No, ma'am," her dad says instantly. "Give her." "But Daddy"

"Take it or leave it, Nikki," he says before either her or her mom can say any more. "It's not negotiable."

She sighs softly and then nods. "mine."

Her mom slowly takes three bills out of her bag and hands them to Nikki. "Here. I will leave dinner on the stove for you and some leftovers in the fridge for the weekend."

Nikki smiles. "Thanks, Mom." When she leaves again, her dad turns to her mom with raised eyebrows. "See what I mean?"

ACT III

The party at Nikki's that night is supposed to be just like every other party. Nikki gets ready in her room, in no rush at all to go downstairs. After all, other people seem to be handling letting everyone in just fine. Mostly, her boyfriend Shawn.

Mike, for example, who arrives an hour late. When he shows up, he walks from the living room of the house towards the back door. It's summer, so it makes more sense for everyone to have the party outdoors. As soon as Mike starts to see people from the party, his mind starts to go a bit haywire.

"Hold on, I'm too live right now. The party is outside. I don't know what y'all doing in here." He isn't really speaking to anyone until his eyes land on a group of young ladies.

"Oh, but then again, I see this
is where all the dry and sexy at. Understood.
How y'all doing?"

There are four girls in the group, and
all of them roll their eyes. "Fine," one says
"That y'all are. Why y'all aint got no drinks
in y'all hands?"

The same one shakes her head.
"Ugh, do we have to drink to party?"

"I mean, look around," he says,
gesturing towards the nearby windows
which show all the partygoers outside.
"Ain't that what everybody doing?

"We different, boo," she says. "We
don't follow trends."

He laughs, quick and loud. "Dang,
I'm just saying. Live a little cause most
people die a lot."

Some of the ladies in the group start to laugh, except for the one who's been speaking to him.

"Okay Drake! How bout you go get us some drinks then since you so concerned?" she says, her voice sharp and sarcastic.

Mike grins. "I would, but you see, the way my body set up, I was only blessed with two hands. But I would be more than happy to escort y'all lovely ladies over to the drinks…"

This wins a smile from the girl.

"Mhm…boy, you silly."

Still, she offers her arm. The group of girls begin toward the kitchen, Mike in tow. Just as they walk in, they realize they shouldn't have come.

"Alright, Tasha, I'm gonna call you," Shawn says to a girl none of them have ever seen before.

Before Mike can ask anything, Shawn's best friend Jonny nudges his friend's side. "Heads up, bruh, ya girl approaching."

The woman of the hour and the house, Nikki, walks into the kitchen, a cup in each of her hands. Clearly, she was having a bit of a pregame while she was

getting ready upstairs.

"What's up, babe?" Shawn says,

reaching his arm out for her.

Nikki swats it away immediately.

"Who was that girl you was just talking to?"

Shawn puts on an expression of feigned

surprise. "What girl?"

Nikki swats at him again. "Don't

play! The one who just walked away as I

was coming up."

Shawn smacks his teeth and glances

around the kitchen, making brief eye

contact with Mike and the girls around him.

"Oh, that's one of my boys' little sisters. I was telling her to tell him to hit me up. I been tryna get in touch with him for a minute now."

"Hmm…okay," Nikki says, staring off into the distance for a long moment. The pause is dramatic, and everyone else in the room can see how much work it takes for Shawn to hold it together. "But don't none of that matter anyway. This is my party. You see how many people out there? I didn't think this many people was gonna show up."

Shawn smiles and puts his arm around Nikki. She accepts it this time.

"Who wouldn't show up to the baddest girl

in the city's party?" he says.

"Aww babe, you right. But the only

person I really cared about showing up was

you." She gives him a quick kiss and

smiles.

Shawn grins even wider. " Yeah…

So, baby, did you get me what I asked for?"

Nikki looks down and flutters her

eyelashes a bit. "Of course, it's in the

kitchen." She glances down at one of the

cups in her hands and offers it to him. "And

I brought you a little something too."

Shawn takes the cup from her and glances at the liquid inside. "Ight, go get that for me."

Nikki pecks another kiss on his cheek and walks off to the dining room to get another drink for her boyfriend. And when Shawn isn't looking, Mike takes his leave from his group and follows her.

"Nikki!" he says when the two of them reach the dining room, as though he's run into her here entirely by chance. "What's up, girl? How you been?"

Nikki glances up at him and then back down to the table where she fixes her boyfriend's second drink. "Hey Mike. I ain't even know you was back in town."

Mike nods and glances around the room as he does. " Yeah, I just got in yesterday. You know you only know what you wanna know."

Nikki shakes her head and throws her head back to take a shot. Then, she reaches down to the table below her and pops a small handful of white powdery pills. "Yep. That's me."

Mike steps back, his eyes widening a bit. "Woah…you messing with them pills now?"

Nikki narrows her eyes at him for a moment, as though she's not sure she's understanding his comment. Then, she nods slowly. "Yeah, I take a few of them every now and then just to keep my mind at ease. I be stressing a lot. So this how I deal with it. Mike scoffs a bit at this. "Aw, you tripping. That ain't a good look."

Nikki looks back down at the table and then back up at him. "Mike, I ain't worried about that. It ain't nobody business what I do. I'm grown, and my man likes it. So that's all that matters."

Mike takes a step closer to her, and Nikki retreats a step in kind. He steps back where he came from. "Man, listen to how you sound. That ain't even cool. Buddy gotchu out here poppin' pills, drinking lord knows what. This ain't you, Nikki. Or at least the Nikki I know." Nikki smacks her lips. "Mike, people change. I grew up." She looks down at the table once more. "I'm grown now, okay! Not everybody's perfect and can go off to college."

Mike nearly laughs, but instead, his voice takes on another strong edge. "Man, this ain't got nothing to do with being perfect. We both know ain't nobody perfect.

Yeah, I'm in college, but let's not act like

you couldn't be there if you really wanted

to. Just cause you dress a lil different, pop

pills, and got a thug boyfriend who a few

years older than you don't make you

grown." Nikki slams her hands down on the

table. "Mike, you so jealous!"

Mike steps back another step, eyes

wide. "Jealous of what? It's actually sad to

see a woman I care about get so lost."

Nikki turns her head towards him,

her hair flying around her shoulders.

"Hmm…I'm nowhere near lost. I know who

I am and what I need to do to get where I wanna be ….and college just ain't it for me. Come on now, look at me! I have what it takes to be somebody and get paid to be that somebody. Now, you tell me how much money you making going to college!" She laughs at this, but he doesn't.

She narrows her eyes at him as he continues. "So seems to me like if anybody is lost, and let's not forget broke, it's you." Mike shakes his head at this. "Okay, so you got it all figured huh? I'm not tryna argue with you. Just know your worth and what you're capable of is all I'm saying. Don't be so caught up in what looks good cause that might not always be the way. You're young

and beautiful with so many capabilities. I

don't want to see all that go to waste."

Nikki slams down the drink she's

been making and just grabs a handle nearby.

"Whatever." With that, she storms out of the

kitchen in search of Shawn.

When she finds him, he's got his

hand on the waist of another girl, a girl she's

never even seen before.

"Umm…what are you doing?"

Nikki says as she approaches.

Shawn laughs. "What does it look like I'm doing? I'm just trying to enjoy myself."

Nikki shakes her head, squeezing her eyes shut as she does. "You can enjoy yourself without being in every female face that walks by! I'M THE ONLY FEMALE THAT SHOULD HAVE YOUR ATTENTION IN HERE!"

Shawn drops his arm from the other girl and turns towards her, flexing his arms. "You better turn yo damn voice down when you talk to me. Know your place."

"My place," Nikki scoffs. "Uhh…

okay, you right, boo."

She turns on her heel and begins to

walk away as Chris and Steph walk in from

the other room. Before she can even make it

over to greet them, she turns back around

and throws the remainder of her drink on

Shawn.

"I hate you!" she cries out.

Shawn steps back as the brown

liquid soaks the front of his shirt. After a

moment of standing frozen, he swings his

hand out to hit Nikki. His friends grab him

before he can.

"Come on, bruh! Calm down. You

tripping," one of his friends says, trying to

pull Shawn's arm down. "Man,

move, Shawn says, and he storms

off to the kitchen. Steph turns to Chris. "Ima

go check on Nikki."

"Yes, do that," Chris mutters under

his breath.

Steph runs off up the stairs to find

Nikki in her room. And Chris, in the

meantime, approaches the kitchen where

Shawn stands with his friends.

"Where the damn napkins at?"

Shawn calls. "I can't believe this. She got

some nerves."

Poppa chooses this moment to walk

into the kitchen from the backyard. He's just

a bit tipsy, but not much. He makes the

mistake immediately of stepping on

Shawn's shoe.

"Oh snap, my bad," he apologizes

quickly.

"You damn right, yo bad," Shawn

shouts. "You can't see?" Poppa shakes his

head. "I said my bad, dog. Chill."

Shawn rises to his full height at that from where he'd been leaning against the counter. "Chill? Naw, I ain't gone chill. These $200 shoes, partna. You best come up off something before things get real bad for you up in here."

Mike steps forward and puts his hand on Poppa's shoulder at this. "Bro, you good?" "Oh yeah," Poppa says, brushing off his hand. "It ain't no worries my way." Shawn looks between the two. "Y'all think this a game?" Mike looks at Shawn. "Bruh, chill."

Shawn scoffs. "All you youngstas got the game twisted."

Before Poppa can conjure a response, Shawn reaches out to throw a punch. At this, Poppa draws his gun quickly from his hip and cocks it.

ACT IV

What happens next, we can assume.

In the meantime, Steph has been lucky enough to find a crying Nikki the only place she expected to find her: her bedroom, sprawled across her cushions. Nikki is deep into an angry sob by the time Steph makes it into her room.

"Nikki, what happened?" Steph says as she sits down on the bed next to her friend. "Talk to me."

"No!" she cries, burying her head in the blankets. "Leave me alone. You wouldn't understand…"

Steph reaches out and rubs her hand gently against Nikki's back. "Come on, Nikki. You know I'm here for you. Tell me what's going on."

Nikki is still for a moment. A long moment. Then, she props herself up on her elbows. "I just want to be loved by a person the way I love them. Is that too much for a girl to ask for?"

Steph shakes her head with a sad smile. "Of course not, but you have to look for love in the right places. You have to be smart about who you decide to give your heart to."

Nikki sighs. "That's easy for you to say because you have Chris. And even before him, I bet every guy who has talked to you has had some respect for you."

"No, that's not true," Steph said gently. "I had it rough before I met Chris. I been through some things in my past that made me the woman I am today. You have to learn how to distinguish the men from the boys. A guy will only go as far as you let him when it comes to him respecting you. When it starts, he texting you 'good morning' and saying all these nice things throughout the day. Then, after you give him your goodies and your heart, it's a different game. A real man will cherish it and help you get stronger. A boy will use and abuse. I was once told the longer you make a man wait, the more respect he will have for you. That makes sense. If all he wants is sex from you, then he won't stay around too long. You just have to pick and choose and be smart about what you do."

Nikki sighs deeply. "I hear you, girl. It's just…I have put so much time and dedication into him. I refuse just to let him go! He has his good and bad ways, but I mean, that's everybody. Nobody's perfect.

I'm just afraid to start over."

Steph laughs a short laugh. "Start

over, huh? Let me tell you a story about

starting over.

"When I was 13 years old, I was

used and abused." Nikki's eyes widen.

"You had a boyfriend at 13?

"No! Definitely not," Steph says

quickly. "It was my mom's boyfriend."

Nikki reaches up to wipe the tears from her

face. "Aww, Steph, for real?"

Steph swallows and stares down into

the cushions this time. "Yes, I wouldn't

make nothing like this up. He used to come

into my room in the middle of the night. He

would sit on my bed and start to rub on me.

Then he would lay down beside of me and

take my pants off.”

"You didn’t scream?”

“No,” Steph says with a sigh. “I

was scared, and he told me that he would

kill my mom and my brother if I made any

noise. So I would just have to lay there

and cry silently while this man took

advantage of me.”

Nikki shakes her head in awe. “It

didn’t hurt?”

“At first it did, but my body started

to go into shock. I couldn’t feel anything

till it was over. It was like I'd black out, and when he was finished, I would just lay there and cry."

Nikki sits in silence for a long moment, processing the information. "So you never told your mom?"

Steph sighs. "Yes but she didn't believe me. Now that I'm grown and think back on it, I believe she felt I was trying to get at him. She would just call me fast and say I needed to stop making up these stories. She even beat me the second time I spoke on it. So, I left it alone…"

Nikki opens her mouth to respond, but Steph begins to sob, her body shaking with emotion.

"My little brother even walked in once," she continues through tears. "He didn't know what to do. My mom's boyfriend told him to go back to bed. But he just stood there in the doorway and cried. He cried for his sister. He saw I had been telling the truth."

Nikki has never seen her friend cry like this, and she watches with wide eyes. "I am so sorry to hear that, Steph. I would've never thought something like that would have happened to you."

Steph sees Nikki's concerned expression and breathes a deep sigh. She begins to wipe the tears from her face as best she can. "It's cool. I'm over it now. After that happened, I looked at life totally different. I hated all men and didn't want anything to do with them. Then, I started having mood swings and blaming myself.

I was angry and wanted revenge, so as I got older, I started sleeping around with guys and then leaving them, thinking I was breaking they hearts.

But really, I was belittling myself and didn't realize it. It took me a long time before I was able to talk about it to people.

But I just prayed, and God helped me

realize I can't let something that happened

to me stop me from becoming the woman he

I set out to be. It was just a test. I failed at

first and then eventually passed. Now, I am

able to testify. I'm not the only girl that has

been raped. There are a lot of young women

who have been through the same thing and

probably don't have anybody to talk to

about it. I realized I can be the person to

help the next woman or

girl who gets thrown into a situation like

that. I didn't want to start loving men

again. But I did what I had to do."

Nikki nods slowly, admiring her friend's strength. "Yeah, I feel that, girl. That is so crazy. For someone who has been through all that, you carry yourself real well. I appreciate you sharing that experience with me."

Steph smiles in response. "That's why you can't judge a book by its cover. You never know what the person next to you has been through. The only person that walks all 24 hours of each day with us is God."

"I hear that!"

The two sit in silence for a moment, lost in their respective minds. Then, Steph turns to Nikki once more.

"So, what happened?"
Nikki sighs, as if the whole thing is
ridiculous now. "Well, I was being really
dumb and letting this fool play me to my
face. It's sad too because…oh my god,
Mike!"

"What about him?" Nikki shakes her
head. "Me and him just got into an
argument because he was telling me kind
of the same things you're saying to me.
Right before the altercation happened with
my boyfriend. I knew he was speaking real
to me and saying what was right. But I
didn't want to hear it, so I went off on
him."

Steph quirks her lip to one side.
"Aww, Nik, you wrong."

Nikki laughs. "I know. Ima apologize. I just hate how he has a way with words. He always tells you the truth even if it isn't what you want to hear."

Steph grins. "Girl, who you telling? I put up with Chris' 'words of wisdom' every day. You know they just alike in a way."

"Girl, yes," Nikki says as she laughs. "You better than me. I don't know how you do it."

"It's cause I love him," Steph says gently. "And-" Just then, their mutual friend Mary races into the room, throwing open the door. "Hurry Come quick!" she cries, her eyes wild. "Poppa and them just got into it with some boys!"

ACT V

The next morning comes quicker than anybody wants it to. Chris and Poppa arrive at the YDC as they normally do, early enough to get everything set up. Mr. T meets them there, and the boys are stunned by how awake he looks. The two of them are nowhere near ready for the fact that another day has already come.

And Mr. T can tell this.

"Long night, son?" he asks Chris.

"Yes, sir," Chris says with a tired smile. "But it was fun."

Poppa sidles up to the two and throws his arm around Chris' shoulder. "What's up, Mr. T? You got an iPhone charger?"

Mr. T nods and gestures toward the corner. "Look over by that lamp."

"Coo. I appreciate that," Poppa says as he crosses toward the corner.

"My phone been in the dead zone since last night. I'm missing out on all the fees."

Mr. T nods, his expression neutral. "So how did the party turn out that y'all been yapping about?"

"It was cool," Chris says, nonchalant. "I didn't expect that many people to show up though. It was people from all sides of town in there. I even seen Ms. Tracy's son. I think his name is Steven?"

"The tall skinny one?" Mr. T asks "Yep, he was in there with his little crew from Cedar High."

"Oh okay," Mr. T says with a nod. "Yeah, I seen they had a good basketball season this year."

Chris nods without saying anything.

"Did they end up dropping that case on his brother, or is it still pending?" Mr. T says after a moment of reflection.

"I don't even know for sure." Chris shrugs. "Last I heard, they were trying to make him sign for two years just for being in the car."

Mr. T tilts his head to one side. "What do you mean?"

"They saying he is an accessory to the robbery because he can't prove he wasn't with the guys when it happened," Chris says. "The pizza man just told the cop that it was three guys with dark hoodies on.

And Ms. Tracy's son happened to make the third guy when they got pulled over."

Mr. T shakes his head at this.

"That's sad. He shouldn't have even been in the car with them fools. Especially if they were doing dumb things like that. Come on now, who robs a pizza man?"

"No, he wasn't even with them when it happened," Chris says quickly. "They had just picked him up and got pulled over after they dropped the original guy who was with them off. So really it's like he was in the wrong place at the wrong time."

Mr. T stares towards the dark TV for a moment, then at Poppa in the corner. He turns back to his son. "I hear you, but at the end of the day, if he can't prove his innocence, he will just have to face reality and do time. You have to pick and choose your friends wisely. There are consequences for every crime once you get caught. It's all about your choices. If you choose to ride with people that do negative things, expect negative results. He put himself in the situation by getting in the car, knowing those guys were up to no good.

I was just reading an article about

something similar to this: a young man in

Georgia lost his scholarship because he was

driving some friends around who had

marijuana on them. When the cops pulled

them over, nobody wanted to own up. So

since he was driving, they put it on him.”

Chris’ eyebrows shot up. “Man, that’s

crazy.”

“Yep, but it's reality,” Mr. T says with a

sigh. Then, he looks back at the entrance.

“Where is Mike? It isn’t like him to be

running this late. He’s always on time.”

"Like I said Pops, we had a long night." Chris laughs a bit and then stops when he sees his dad's gaze. "I'm just kidding…I'm sure he'll be stumbling in here any minute now."

Just then, the doorbell rings. "I'll get it," Chris says.

"You didn't unlock the front yet?" Mr. T says.

"Not yet," Chris says as he presses the buzzer. "That ain't nobody but Mike anyways."

"You know what time that door is supposed to be unlocked. Don't let it happen again."

Chris begins to respond, but before he can, Nikki storms into the room. And she's sobbing. Chris and Poppa are both completely taken aback.

"Nikki, what's wrong? What are you doing here?" Chris says. She doesn't answer, only continues to cry. Chris asks again.

"Nikki? What's up? Talk to me."

"He's gone," she says through sobs.

"Who?"

"He's gone."

Chris shakes his head, frustrated.

"Who? Nikki, what are you talking about?"

Poppa approaches from the corner, silent and curious. As soon as Nikki catches sight of him, she erupts into another fit.

"It's his fault!" she points at Poppa.

"It's all your fault." Poppa shakes his head.

"Girl, what you talking about?"

She doesn't pay any mind to his words.

"You always have to be the big tough guy on the scene. Can't nothing just be handled with conversation with you."

Chris steps forward towards Nikki.

"Please tell me what you're talking about."

"It's Mike," she spits out. "He's been shot."

Chris turns towards Poppa with wide eyes.

"Shot?"

Nikki can hardly get the words out.

"Yes, after y'all left. We were just there

cleaning and talking. Everything was going fine until my ex showed back up. He started tripping on me bad, pulling me by my hair out the house. Mike ran out, tried to save me. The next thing I knew, he was on the floor, gasping for life."

Chris couldn't believe his ears. "He's okay though, right?"

"I don't know," Nikki cries. "I have been at the police station all night. They didn't let me call anybody. Y'all are the first people I've been able to talk to. I just know they took him to Saint Luke Hospital on Third Street in critical condition."

Poppa stares around the room, eyes wide. "SO YOU'RE TELLING ME MY BROTHA GONE?" When no one responds, he continues. "NAW, NAW, MAN, I AIN'T TRYNA HEAR THAT!"

He is the first to run out of the room and find his way to the hospital. The others aren't far behind.